NATIONAL
GEOGRAPHIC

Bicycles

Gare Thompson

Introduction

Today, you can ride all kinds of bikes. You can ride a racing bike. You can ride a mountain bike.

You can ride a bike in different places. You can ride a bike on a road. You can ride a bike in the park. Bikes today are very different from the bikes of long ago.

Early Bicycles

In Germany, a man built a two-wheeled walking machine in 1816. It was made of wood. It had no pedals. You moved the two-wheeler by walking it. You steered with a bar connected to the front wheel.

Riding a walking machine ▶ was a bit like using a scooter.

4

The first bikes were made of wood. They did not have pedals.

Over time, inventors improved these early wooden bikes. They added pedals and a steering fork. These things helped to move and steer the bike.

Later, they added metal tyres. Riders shook as they rode the bikes with metal tyres over the bumpy streets. They called these bikes "boneshakers".

steering fork   pedal

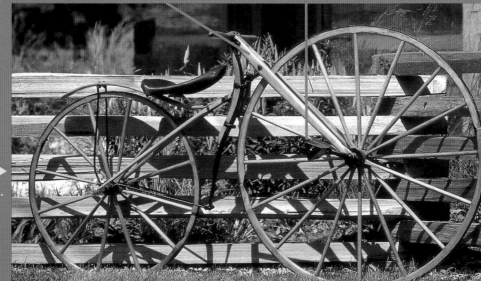

"Boneshakers" were ▶ not comfortable to ride.

The next bike was called a "penny-farthing". Pedals were attached to the large front wheel. The wheel was large to make the bike go faster. The larger the wheel, the faster the bike could go.

The penny-farthing bike was popular in the 1880s. ▶

The Modern Bicycle

In 1886, a bike manufacturer in England made the first safety bike. Safety bikes looked much like the bikes we ride today. The safety bike had wheels that were the same size. The pedals were attached to a chain. Now, a rider could use the pedals to move the back wheel.

solid rubber tyres

chain

1880s

Bicycle Changes Over Time

changing gears

racing handlebars

light frame

drink holder

1940s   1960s 1970s   Today

reflector   headlight

elevated seat

thicker tyres for riding cross country

9

Bicycles Became Popular

The safety bike made riding easier and safer.
By the 1890s, bikes were becoming very popular.
More and more people bought bikes. Soon, the
streets were filled with people riding bikes to
and from work. Riders formed bike clubs.
Others began to race.

A boy practises riding ▶
at bicycle school in 1961.

At first, women wore long skirts when riding bikes. Their skirts would get caught on the bar. Bike manufacturers started to make bikes for women to ride. These bikes did not have a bar across the top.

▲ Many women rode three-wheelers in the 1890s.

▼ By 1936, many women wore shorts when cycling.

11

Bicycles at Work

People use bikes for many different reasons. Many people use bikes for work. Some use bikes to deliver groceries. Couriers use bikes to deliver packages. Police use bikes, too.

These police patrol on bikes. ▶

In some parts of the world, taxi drivers use bikes.
A bike taxi has a large seat at the back for passengers.
The taxi driver pedals the bike.

▲ Bike taxis are common in Asia.

Riding Bicycles for Fun

Many people ride bikes for fun and sports. In cities, bike paths have been built so people can ride their bikes safely.

People ride bikes for exercise, too. They ride to stay fit and healthy. They ride outside or they ride indoors on exercise bikes.

Some people race bikes. One of the most famous bike races is the Tour de France. This race across France lasts three weeks.

Tour de France riders race through Paris, France. ▶

15

Bike Safety

Bikes are a great way to get around. They don't make the air dirty. They are good exercise. So put on your helmet and start pedalling!

As you ride, remember to be safe.

◆ Use hand signals.

◆ Obey all traffic signs.

◆ Keep to the left. Ride in the direction the traffic is going.

◆ Obey local bike laws.

◆ Watch out for potholes and other road problems.

◆ Have fun, but pay attention.

Hand Signals

Left turn

Right turn

Stop or slow